The Grammar of Distance

The
GRAMMAR OF DISTANCE

Poems

IAN BURGHAM

Tightrope Books

Tightrope Books
602 Markham Street
Toronto, Ontario
Canada M6G 2L8
www.tightropebooks.com

Canada Council
for the Arts

Conseil des Arts
du Canada

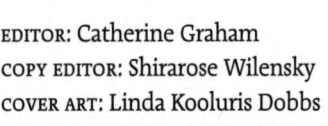

ONTARIO ARTS COUNCIL
CONSEIL DES ARTS DE L'ONTARIO

EDITOR: Catherine Graham
COPY EDITOR: Shirarose Wilensky
COVER ART: Linda Kooluris Dobbs
COVER DESIGN: Karen Correia Da Silva
TYPESETTING: Shirarose Wilensky

Produced with the assistance of the Canada Council for the Arts, the Ontario Arts Council, and Maclean Dubois.

Printed in Canada.

Distributed in the United Kingdom by Maclean Dubois, Hillend House, Hillend, Edinburgh, EH10 7DX.

LIBRARY AND ARCHIVES CANADA CATALOGUING IN PUBLICATION

Burgham, Ian
      The grammar of distance / Ian Burgham.

Poems.
ISBN 978-1-926639-09-3

      I. Title.

PS8603.U737G73 2009   C811'.6   C2009-906627-0

Also by Ian Burgham

A Confession of Birds

The Stone Skippers

Praise for *The Stone Skippers*:

"There's exceptionally thoughtful and complex writing here, writing that always seems willing to enter emotions with great courage and finesse. I admire the honesty. The poems are genuinely moving."
—BARRY DEMPSTER

"I admire *The Stone Skippers* greatly. The poems have a hardness and succinctness. This concision, leanness, and directness, brings out the emotion in them, the sense of distance and space and wind-sweep both emotional and imagistic, wonderfully well. There are poems that stay with one. There are many items of praise I could include, but just let me say, Burgham has written a good book, and good poems!"
—A.F. MORITZ

"*The Stone Skippers* is a rare volume: a book filled with generous emotion as well as craft and polish. What is said is as important as how it is said. Each line break, each simile, each rhythmic construct: all these things display both care and wisdom, and that's a treasure."
—CAROLYN SMART

"Here's a gifted new poet, madly dashing his love-torn heart against the poetic stones of the universe. Impetuous, inspired, wild, unadorned, unrepentant, desperate, occasionally eloquent—this is a voice you don't want to miss. Ladies and gentlemen, Mr Ian Burgham."
—DI BRANDT

"Here is a writer capable of great subtlety, fusing the turning point moment of short story, depth and length of novel, 'in-breath' of exalted verse. Use of form, poetic device, economy, and choice of language, blurring of fancy and fiction—all are employed with intelligence and readerly insight. Burgham demonstrates the dancing quality and length of well-crafted poetry . . . The poems are to be savoured, lingered over, allowed to resonate and be remembered. Strongly recommended!"
—KEVIN GILLAM, *Five Bells*, Australian Poets Union

"I feel a great sense of discovery. These poems mark the emergence of a mature and distinctive poetic voice. The language is sure and elegant; most importantly, it is infused with a quiet musicality that is a rare and remarkable gift. This is the work of one who has the ear for the possibilities of language."

—ALEXANDER MCCALL SMITH

"*The Stone Skippers* is a wonderful collection that needs to be read over and over again. I often judge the worth of poems by my own willingness to return to a book. I enjoy a wide range of poetry and poets but there are only a few books that I keep close so that I can re-read them when I need them. And it is a need—they serve a purpose at times when you want to know how another person has given a new perspective, has caught the world in an image that you can carry around with you, that satisfies something within. *The Stone Skippers* is such a book."

—ROLAND LEACH

"*The Stone Skippers* is a wonderful, terrible collection, and a pleasure to read."

—CHRISTINA DECARIE, *The Antigonish Review*

To Allen and Jean Burgham

CONTENTS

BLOOD AND BONE

We go into distances, near or far, each man to his own bourne.

George MacKay Brown
"Foresterhill"

. . . and nothing to show for the journey from nowhere to here.
Not what you had hoped for: no answer, no transformation,
Only a man your age, like your father before you
Standing alone in the hallway, your father's father . . .
that grammar of distance and blood.

John Burnside
"Alcools"

FOREWORD

Poetry: A High-Risk Activity

> Tonight a poet, deep in a bed of black,
> mills these silences roaring with
> stars in the heights of heavens . . .
> —Ian Burgham, "The Mill at Eyrland"

Reviewers of Ian Burgham's first poetry collection, *The Stone Skippers*, were struck by the eloquence of the writing, its "hardness and succinctness," and its emotional courage. As Di Brandt put it, "here's a gifted new poet, madly dashing his love-torn heart against the poetic stones of the universe. Impetuous, inspired, wild, unadorned, unrepentant, desperate . . . eloquent . . . a voice you don't want to miss." Clearly, Burgham set the bar high for himself in his first book and he sets it equally high in this, his second collection. He soars over it easily, yet it should not be inferred from this that Burgham takes his poetic vocation lightly. Making a poem is, on the contrary, a high-risk activity, a "grim compulsion," as he writes in "Sometimes." Poems, for Ian Burgham, are a matter of life and death—at the very least, an act of utter immersion, a journey to the self's darkest places.

Burgham writes from his gut and his heart. His imagery is, by turns, sensuous and rough-hewn, soft and hard. "The buttered moon comes knocking" delineates the contrary states that are often in play in his work. I wasn't surprised to discover that Ian is a musician. His poems crackle with sonic energy; they whinny and stamp. They whistle in the dark. His poetic landscapes frequent the windswept coasts of Scotland; but in this collection, we also find him doing terribly Canadian things like snowshoeing, surveying, chopping wood. I sometimes hear Al Purdy in Burgham's voice and, occasionally, Patrick Lane. Fists are known to fly in Burgham's poems, and the writing is often marked by a visceral quality. His penchant for storytelling and Celtic elegiac moods makes him a solid candidate for the position of poetic counterpart to Alistair MacLeod. Gut and heart, yes. But Burgham is also a thinker, a philosophical poet. A restless soul who asks big questions; an example from "The Falcon" illustrates this: " . . . where is the place that serves silence, / the rare stillness, the rescue from despair?"

Burgham's literary influences range far and include William Blake, Tomas Transtromer, Sorley MacLean, W.H. Auden, and Simon Armitage, among others. Like all strong poets, his imagination breaks past borders. Tribal and intense, Ian's poems are conversations with loved ones, lost ones, and all the poets with storms in their bones. They are feisty. They rant. They grieve. They celebrate. I admire his refusal to shy away from emotional excess, and his willingness to embrace all manner of the heartland's hazards and risks. I admire equally his willingness to tackle, head on, the sheer inescapable fact of our aloneness in this world, and our inevitable fallibility as humans—our brilliance at messing things up. Despite this, Ian's vision is one of compassion; and poetry for him, is a seeing beyond "the limits / of our poor decisions."

Happily for us, Ian Burgham follows his lyric muse unabashedly. He lets 'er rip and takes his poems where they need to go, full-tilt, and "roaring with stars." When it comes to the poetic vocation, Burgham is a star. And he's roaring.

Jeanette Lynes
ANTIGONISH, NOVA SCOTIA

LOVE FORTHWITH

Music of a Walk Through Leaves

We'd walk home from school, hand in hand,
through the music of fallen leaves,
the girl whose family owned the dairy.
She took piano lessons and sang in the choir.
She could raise a spring day with her song.
Sing the losses in me. Re-tune the world.

Since stepping ashore from the ship that
sometimes fuelled my dwindling dreams,
carrying my diminished life in a backpack,
providing my own running commentary to fill the silence,
I've revisited our walk over the years since she left,
trying to find the music of those leaves.
No trace, a random arrangement of notes.

Picture a grown man on leave from his senses,
testing his iron will, the thrust of his hands
through dead duff. Off in the harbour distance,
beyond arm's length, the ship's blasting horn,
if you see what I mean.

Raven Dreams

I don't give a damn if she likes this poem or not.
I wrote it when the heat of a dream was over me,
reaching for her shoulders, her waist,
and pulling her to me hoping she wakes
in the night with a gasp, feels cold shock,
that kind that sends pins and needles down her spine.

I hope she loses sleep from my raven dream,
the black weight of a bird's body, soft imprint
from a fan of feathers, the hint of perfect wings
on last night's snow, the embossing kiss of
a sudden lift into the sky—a frozen memory,
the impression of a perfect snow angel.

In the heat of sun, heaven's form expands,
draws itself awake in the melt of light
into something fierce, dangerous—
innocence undone by dawn.

The Snow Garden at Massey College

A woman stands at the window transfixed by
the thought that, though it's made of millions
of crystals, new snow looks empty,
like the sheet on her half-made bed,
only one impression.

Through tears she looks for an interruption,
a kind of sign, an understanding from watching the light
break apart in tiny prisms of snow crystals,
the physics of refraction. Her husband's absence
has left the beginnings of a long ache.
She looks for the way you find yourself
when you're no longer looking.
She looks to find the way light rejoins
after it shatters, splits.

I'd like to help her but no one can save you
from your life. And I can't remember anything
about prisms and light. All I know is there's
no mercy to be found in times like these,
no profit in advice, no answers.
Just see it through, this common loneliness.
You have to. It's such a long distance to love,
and it doesn't answer that question.

Eden

Not counting everything else that day,
I remember having handed you an apple.
One bite and you threw it at me,
along with various accusations.
Nothing left unsaid. Everything meant.

It was cold-hearted of me, to say the least.
Or maybe exploitation on my part,
self-indulgence, self-flagellation,
obsession, but I kept the fleshy core.
Your teeth marks were a transient imprint
in the flesh of what became this poem.

Our Lady of Montreal

Languid nights the length of limbs,
cathedral heights the distant depths of rivers,
rope her hair, hand over hand a bell-ringer monk,
ailing lover, climbs the dark for salvation
in the staring silence between the intoning bells—
eye to eye with God.

In last night's dark, dark inward tolling
through all the stations of the cross that
threaded Côte St. Antoine, he wrote the
pure cold note of November, a wintry
wordless psalm of wounds to call forth the world:
Our Lady, is there really too much in the way?
Accept a lover's risk.
My art, my life, my answer, my prayer
that holy love can't go wrong.
His mouth still tastes the juice of crushed kisses,
the private wine of Bar Alexandre
where the world walked in from frozen streets,
turned to hang their coats,
stood envious of her holiness in him
as she descended the crescendo of stairs.

He asks her: *Notre Dame, can you*
grant grace, choice, life?
Can we hold immaculate proximity
with that mysterious care,
the lodestone of glorious necessity,
the rock to moss,
our earth to the sun,
the thief to Jesus upon his wooden cross?

Or is past, present, and future only loss?
Our Lady, lose yourself. By the back door
of holy mother moon leave the mountain
of your supposed assumption for mad minutes
in the steps of the temple's maze so lost on others.
They have no inspiration, those who run from death.

He holds her with words that represent no thing but
purity straight from the soul, feet against feet,
spoon in spoon, his bared left leg looped in love
over hers—prayer, altar to Notre Dame,
begin a new past forge-fired in a naked flame.
He's crying for what didn't last, not unhappy
but not forgetting the past pain of living,
its continuing muscular dread.

You're thinking I wrote this about me. I didn't.
Tonight is a black toothless mouth, though I have
the company of sad Sulpicians, so separated from him,
black clad, walking east on Michel Saint Martin,
chanting: *Pray for us*—their tired tolling bell:
This life, that one, what we can't have, what we will.

Act Three

Life departs past the Victory Café,
the sinews of summer-sunned legs,
her stubborn hair perfection.

She's passed across the skies,
like no one else of earth,
through the burden of living,

He stares down at his beer.
At his age, especially his age,
he ignores what he knows—
how life contracts.

Symptoms

Damn right, I have some—
mood at war with spirit.
And I'm not taking the good advice offered.
I'm thinking of my lover tonight.
I've got a hunch this is the moment.
She's uncaptured. I'm in captivity
but ready to be on the loose, stick my neck out.
I'd risk an angry kiss upon the bull's nose
if I thought it would change the world
to what it should be.

She is my existence,
the bones of my bones.
So to hell with thought.
This is a charging wish.
These are grave ambitions.
I'm a hard grip, a tight fist.
My fingernails are cutting
through my hands.
This is that small moment
before the world breaks down.
If she arrives now, I think
we'll get away with this.

Tonight There's Only Absence

It was different last year, walking Sauzet's
dark streets, creating history, the traffic of
conversation connecting us as the moon
pulls the sea. Each night, everything conspired
to make living what it should be.
Apples were apples in the sleeping orchards—
you commented on their perfect appleness,
placed the tips of your fingers into the
pin-pricked cloth of sky and said:

> *Stars are moving away from us.*
> *You can't measure those disappearing distances.*
> *If you could, you'd measure the distance to eternity.*

We held tightly to each other
with the necessity of earth to sun.

This May Not Be Love

My plan was to map her beauty while she slept,
write a poem with conviction,
paying strict attention to geography.
Instead, I sat in the shadows.
I couldn't write—
her silhouette and breathing messed my plans.

Now from a lack of courage—
no poem ever came from a coward—
I was facing the long night of regret.
Feelings unsealed.
How easy it was to become my own enemy.
Across the room, dull stone eyes.
Then, arching like a cat,
the sudden traffic of her stare.

Out of the Beaks of Birds

Night and the world through windows—
ribs of rain and sleet on the pane,
the wind a shout from the grave of the sea.
I'm skull and eyes over your sleep trying to
track you down, but in the deep of existence
you're hiding your soul.

If I shake you awake you'll hear the grief-shrieks
of gulls. But will you hear the sighs from
the hard mouth of the moon? See angels
walk out of the wounds of waves?
See the fire flower with roses?

Listen! The music's rolling up from a soul,
the rising slow, and calling out
through the beaks of birds.
And the sea has become choice.

Birds in a Cage, Canaries in a Mine

Our normal walk through begging streets,
tickets issued by the uniformed, the guy
on the bike through the red light yelling
at the car that blasts its horn, both claiming
ownership of the world.

But swallows inhabit the deeps of our pockets.
Sometimes in the most hopeful of dreams,
like when we first fall in love, they escape,
flutter for a moment on the stoop of our tongue
sweet as a kiss, then swoop,
slice the water's skin, slim wingtip touch,
comet's tail of dust falls from wings.

Feathered now, desire takes flight
with the glorious urgency of pointless resolve,
barrelling on through despair,
undressing desolation, the bitter solitude
of a moth amongst roses, those nights
when not even the cellphone can
put us in touch with someone else.

The birds of possibility bring light.
The sun shines, burns the skin of buildings.
Bedsheets on clotheslines flap greetings
behind the tenements. Separation, betrayal—
never happened.

Lies don't exist when two bite into inclination,
meet beyond halfway, demand nothing,
and kiss to birth the world.

Things true become themselves—red as roses,
blue a deeper glory than the sky.
And chairs at the café whistle, invite,
Raise a glass with us.

Later they rise; the morning birds call for connection—
who's dead, who's still here, who's survived the night.
Do you love me?
I need to be alone.
The conference starts soon. Get your own meal.
I'll be back tomorrow.
These are bird songs too.

A Body Translated

From Lust to Long-legged Emotion by a Middle-aged Man

She sits across from me at Starbucks.
It is the landscape of her foot (which I think
no one has ever visited) and soft hint of where
the September channels of erosion will form
above her lip when she is ripe and singing,
and those wild weeds of April hair.
If I could get to know her, together our
summer breath might make hours of clouds,
and August kisses become roses
flowering in our mouths,
before the pinch of frost begins.

Hearts is Trump

They played till the night became too long.
They had worked out signals for a winning hand.
She took her lead from the foot under the table.
Her husband and the neighbour's wife played
their hands oblivious to what might be,
their "bid and ask," a kind of dance.

Underneath thin marriages, a heavy weight
bearing down on worthy existence, a quiet game
of vehemence in the midst of an enemy, or
from inner weather, the insistence of necessary.

Once It Gave Me Words

> You showered hope upon me and desire
> In our last moment, ere we came to part;
> And then the wind blew all your words away.
> —Petrarch, Sonnet 228

It doesn't make me happy to tell you this
but insurance tables don't lie.
They reveal a deal with the devil.
I can put on a brave face,
but I begin to see a foreigner in me.
It no longer matters if I tick things
off the list of what I need to do
that are never going to happen.
Time has become a unit of decay.

I still want to believe I burn in you.
But I know the worst, recognize
it has nothing to do with death.
It has to do with ransacking that
drawer of the past, being reminded
I've been deprived of you,
catching glimpses of us behind my eyes
in the hatched green of a spruce bud,
the smell of woodsmoke,
in the taste of a gin and lemon.

Breath of Life

For Tamas

Rather than think about arguments over money,
contributions to the local economy,
the sulfur-smell of our well water,
the disappearance of my wife from my life
taking history with her,
I want a tightfisted belief to hold on to.

For reasons I don't know, I begin with the name
of an absent friend, one who knows her well.
I disturb his sleep with a one-sided conversation,
hoping he doesn't miss the point,
gets past old grudges, sees it my way.
I tell him she's left. I think he knows,
in spite of my silliness, I've always meant well.

Talking to him I relax behind my rib cage,
lean against my backbone, breathe
in that moment when you know
long love for another lessens the blow,
becomes enough to get you through disappearance.
He would tell you the same thing.

The View From Here

I've thought about it often,
more since the rust has been eating away.
I'm starting to look worn and thin.
Pilot light's on, the fuel is low.
Still out there round the town,
wearing a number of hats,
going by several names,
not letting the side down,
meet the guys at the pub,
exchange views on hockey, politics,
stay off the subject we all stay away from,
watch the construction workers across the street
make the mistakes we invent for them:
Shouldn't be using a nail gun there,
that's going to pull apart, one of us says,
the rest nod wisely, stay long enough
to get a little drunk, head home to crash early.

That's when they surface—grains of the past.
Nothing I can do.
I work hard to deal with memories,
take off the blindfold, face them.
I'm brought to a night when I made love
to a woman I'd pursued for years.
Uneasy recollection.

Understand, I knew she had no intention of
following through on kissed promises.
We had agreed what the terms were.
Problem was, I had hoped she was a liar,
a promise breaker. But then, years later
I'm still trying to forgive the two of us.

I look for something sweet that might
have been won, left behind.
Even by mistake some good can come.
But one can risk too much
in that desire for intimacy.
Still, I'm working on living with it,
moving through versions of me
from alias to alias,
no longer trying to tow the line.

Edinburgh: City of Enlightenment

I remember what I didn't do at Edward's party.
She invited me right there on the turnpike stair
to hike her skirt and take her in a brawl.
A heat-wave, fire-wild in winter.

All fingers and eyes, we danced close, as though
to bleed each other. I had moved against her.
She had pressed back a tight energy that left space
only wide enough for dreams to slip through.

And I didn't, for whatever intrusive reason,
or moment of sense or stupid pause,
allow the two of us to make music in that place.
We were two distinct inhabitants. I wasn't prepared
to share that gape of space between our bodies.
She didn't ignore the declaration.

Now, thinking of where I didn't go,
I do what I agreed I'd never do,
regret what I can't have back—continually
ask the secret questions I have lived with since:
what was there, what might have been, what lacked.

Shoot the Moon

Because the world has symptoms,
and love has moods and my mind
won't leave me alone, I've cleaned
the lens of the rifle's site.
She's not here on the very night
the whole world has fallen.
So I'm putting things to the test.
I've got the crosshairs trained
on a crater on the moon.
I'm going to shoot it up.
I'm going to alter its face.
Test my aim, a measure of purpose.
The moon's a dead stone.
There'll be no one to blame.

There are times when you need
to consider the worst to pick up
hints of the better, start something
that can't be finished, even if you're
not going to get away with it.
The katydid on the window screen seems
certain someone will answer.
He rasps for connection,
spins the bottle on the silence.
I don't have that insect confidence.
She makes a habit of being away on nights like this.
My shout, my last attempt, as though
I call from the South Pole: no directions
no matter which way I shout, no answers.
No echoes move about.
I hope a gunshot will get a response.

She's away on nights when, pivoting,
my mind teeters.
The only direction is up,
if I believe such direction exists.
And just in case she might hear,
the crosshairs are trained
on an astonished moon,
the dark crater
of my face.

Sheet Lightning

It used to be our clouds collided,
electrons—ecstatic and charged—
in love's slow grind and separation.
The way it was till you forgot to be there,
until from the same force field
another pushed pale lightning
through the storm of your hair.

Now, where are we?

No other lover but me could launch
such super-heated light through this
tempest of separating hearts,
these clouded remains.

The Savage God

For Al Alvarez

> Kisses leave no fingerprints.
> —Lawrence Durrell, "Chanel"

In an otherwise emptied night, deep
in that low pressure of absence,
you no longer a story unfolding,
just a dark figure naked in damp shadows,
immersed in worship to a savage god.

She came disguised as love,
knew how to satisfy a man
for the hell of it—run roughshod.
But you found out.
Unfaithfulness put pressure on a hair trigger.

This morning, on the bridge above,
commuters shiver in heavy traffic—
the decent lightweights, the rest of us,
wretched, oblivious to what has happened,
radios cranked to catch the morning news,
up to our armpits in small concerns,
crawling towards our own end of life.

All and All

> Be patient. Sit motionless before a page
> That holds the image of a face, its questions
> Answered by the May sky's deepest blue;
> Or put it down to age, or the way time feels as it passes.
> —John Koethe, "Piranesi's Keyhole"

It doesn't matter who went first, the feeling's
recognizable—adrift, free. I know this inward place—
I just can't show you. It happens to everyone,
some before death, some after. Sooner or later
love gets rough, goes wrong, comes undone.
Loneliness becomes routine.

Some nights I set sail into isolation,
move out into heavens held in the mind,
held by the sea, framed by calm memory
and thoughts of the view from the window
of a house at Margaree.
Silence is source; the quiet the meaning.

But hurt is source as well.
At least, I think it might be.
And I can't live apart from thoughts of you
having rubbed shoulders with me.
We're in this together.

Tonight the setting isn't as sublime as
the Margaree tide line, though the sun's
sending sea-light from somewhere into the moon's face.
I'm adrift between stars, walking
in the melt and snow on College Street,
heading to the bar for a drink.

A drink for me, to you, and to the memory
of those old inshore fishermen who endure
lonely lives in tide-talk after the death of love.
In a ceremony of sorrow they sit in the Bluefin Bar
and remember the slant of light, conjure
leaping memories of silvered fish
in the spindrift talk, and maintain a belief
in the same bittersweet wave-dance
as you in me.

Not My Wish

At this time in my ancient life,
though it's not my wish,
I give up hope of travelling together
and depart from you to hurtling skies of physics,
a mad mass of molecules that becomes light
of whereabouts, the clock measurement
of day to night and dawn again—
not divine, not human, invented.

Time began and it will end.
But you will only repeat love.

DEEP IN THE EYE

The Falcon

This is the still centre, an involvement in silences.
—Al Purdy, "Winter Walking"

. . . and in despair
only to think of you and you were there.
—Lawrence Durrell, "Deus Loci"

I was staying at the Haven Hotel
within a quick grab of the sea.
The wind backed, rustled the salt grass.
The storm broke in fistfuls.
A torn sea rolled night on its side.
Black waves of unknowns rushed
frantic to find me in possession
of the act I can never let go.

A falcon, from an unseen fist, mantled my work.
Even in the middle of such a wide-awake dream,
life is out of season—the bitter balance of
destruction, creation.

So where is the place that serves silence,
rare stillness, the rescue from despair?
Unhooded, unmanned, seeing you dressed
in ungloved words, towering to rain down
in the sudden bolt of a bird.
Pure rain. Strikes everywhere.

The Mill at Eyrland

Mapped with moods
the buttered moon comes knocking.
The millstone no longer grinds its teeth.
Unheard, a fist of wind stirs pools of wheat,
moves on the barley sea.

Tonight a poet, deep in a bed of black,
mills these silences roaring with
stars in the heights of heavens,
while the dead around him lie in their absence,
now full, now ended.

The Dead

> We are born with the dead.
> —T.S. Eliot

Jamie MacLean's been spotted again up by the old wharf.
Same place he was seen last time,
down the road from where he lived.
Trouble is he's been dead since 1943.
Drowned at sea.

The broken circuit in time doesn't seem to worry anyone.
This countryside is deep-peopled in dead under grass mounds,
and everyone knows that the drowned do turn up.

Beyond the clotheslines of waving bedsheets holding on tight,
the flap of fishermen's yesterdays, childhoods,
and the anxious print dresses of wives,
the sea becomes the curiosity of others,
who each graveyard ocean wave has become. No war
ever ended for those who sleep with water for breath.
The dead continue to rub and salt their bones in
the wet tongues of tides, float in the landwash,
keep secrets of the water.

The doors of the crofts are always open.
The villagers are not afraid to stare the dead in the face.
The dead have their job to do.
Country people weigh the counsels of ghosts,
with their deep sea-wrinkled faces, thin sightseers.
They are beyond the limits of our poor decisions—
remind us we're bigger than our losses.

From time to time men who drown
come home on a stingray's wing
for tea and eggs.

The Walk to Plockton Cemetery

There was nothing to do or say.
Even the dogs stopped their hoarse barking.
Words stood still.
Words emptied.
We dreamed emptiness.

Sam's poems mend our selves,
make us know just who we are.
But we were asking tougher questions:
Who abandoned whom?
Where will words come from for mending?
For some trouble?
Stir up heavy weather?

Following the hearse past the Haven Hotel
a wind-song began in the wires above our heads.
The sound of him turning in me, colliding,
a voltage strike to the bone, something
which contained his answer—those left behind
will write what won't be unspoken.

The barometer's needle was falling fast.
Storms were moving into poets' bones.

Surveying

Man, we were force. We were walking out. Nine days, twelve-hour ones, cutting line so we could make out the plumb string over the smallest point on earth from the lens of the theodolite 900 yards away. All that to tie some guy's cottage land into the evenly divided world. His place and some border in Nepal were always in the same relation to each other. We cut line in spite of some high-school-teacher cottager yelling at us to leave nature alone, "You barbarians!" and threatening to call the police. After Bob told him to screw off we all got on with the steel-fuelled job of trees and rock. Bob had said the right thing, but I saw him cut the head off a snapping turtle with brushcutters—from living thing to dead so fast I feared it, not how quickly it could come, but how some of us are.

The best part, the dark ache in our growing muscles. When you're out in the bush you grow invincible. Learn to like war on your bone-broken body, and you're bloody well in a war in the bruise-high heat of summer north of Parry Sound. Black flies. Mosquitoes. Bug juice all over our glistening bodies. Cigarettes. An attitude. And each of us tough as hunger, savage, fine and muscular, glowing and wet with sweat through a skin stretched tight over rock-ribs of moving muscle.

Unrepentant, we move out after nine days carrying twenty-eight pounds of instruments, tripod, axes, brushcutters, iron bars, machetes, camping gear. When you sweat you watch it run over your muscles. Your body hurts like it's ripping, the mind has stopped making itself up. A wound. Atrophy. The game each night to place the lit cigarette on each other's shoulder, see who gives up first.

In the truck, we pound down the asphalt on the way back to a re-entry we didn't want to make. The road mile markers aren't evenly spaced. Thoughts are different as we approach each one. Get to it, move away. The speed is relative and so are the miles because of what the mind has become during this deep-veined return.

The Michelangelo Code

Based on the Sistine Chapel panel, The Creation of Adam

I

The first man Adam was made a living soul;
the last Adam was made a quickening spirit.
—I Corinthians 15: 45

And God said, let us make man in our image,
after our likeness, in the image of God created he him . . .
And the Lord God formed man . . . and breathed into his nostrils
the breath of life; and man became a living soul.
—Genesis 1: 26, 27

You slap down the Euros (knowing you're
the sick worm within the apple) and make
for the chapel—the new Pope, speaking with
an affectionate tongue, hasn't been whipped (yet),
and the business guys in dog collars still run the
basilica kiosks with brooding holy lust.
One ecumenical priest has the franchise
for circumcisions, another for reattachments—
human error, free will.
Quilts are sold made entirely of the Pope's robe,
postcards from photographs of the crucifixion.

Looking up into the chapel ceiling long enough
to dream our origin in this strange constellation,
you've arrived at the moment of life. What was lost,
in a kind of innocence, as though you have walked
barefooted through dead leaves in the spring woods.
You see evidence in the draped shape of the dead
before touch, the limp hand twisted, a body lying

lifeless before the power of the unfolding hand to
make a living soul. That fixed break. That baffling
space between life and death. The Word and Adam,
the namer of all things, the divide between the thing
and the vital. This drop-off distance between the
light and the dark, before time began to run down.

Here you are, Michelangelo, lying nose against ceiling,
creating the moment before creation, painting
the gap between the shell and the turtle's flesh.
Wedged between scaffolding and the ceiling plaster,
drawing breath, measuring the design of Heaven and Hell,
our ignorant distress between the two in this graffiti.

II

> Hereafter shall you see the Son of man
> sitting on the right hand of power,
> and coming in the clouds of heaven.
> —Matthew 26: 64

Tourist. Little *homo sapien*. Holy Namer.
Here you dream the moment of death
before life and useless thoughts.
The evidence for this?
Twist of the sinister wrist,
the wrist of the human Christ
twisted by the weight of the world.
Here is the lifeless hand of the first Adam.
Here the witness of inevitable wounds, a body
tearing itself down by its own weight,
flesh shreds against resisting nails.
Why hast thou forsaken me?
Our own accusation.
In the shape of hanging and limp,
this left arm and left hand, mirror of the right,
though you share both, Son of God, Son of man.
The hands—dexterous—and sinister—crucified;
to man, mariner of mute space between heaven and earth.

III

Death belongs to us in that distant vacuum.
Separation of hand and finger to hand and finger,
that baffling space, the place at which all clocks stop.
The place of connection between faithlessness and grace,
hope and hopelessness, the living and the dead;
the power of God when you are man, and your body
filled with the failure of worlds at the moment when
sun and stars disappeared, darkness appeared over the world
and the death was mutual.

The bold right hand, image of the left,
The dexterous hand of our divinity,
the source to alter a starless sky.
The power of invention to make a living soul
reaches across the fear of being alone—the precipice—
only to touch the space of separation, to impart the beginning
with the force from a finger making dead bones dance.
This equilibrium of arm and hand, gentle equation of life and death;
crux of harmony in the midst of vast distance,
melody between son and father that answers all riddles.
Defeats death. Defeats religion.

Hey, priest! Magician!
While your guests fidget with their cellphones,
your law, your commerce, guts the bellies of the citizens.
For the sorry believers caught by the priestly infection
of Sin and stern Repentance, the day dies.
Dark clouds carry tears for the living who,
unlike you, cannot speak beyond knowledge,
and don't know that Death has been swallowed
the way you swallow his melting body
in the wafer you made.

IV

Or is there sanctuary for those who realize the right
hand is their own stretching out across a narrow sea?
It's priests, it's that faith, which populates hell—
the peopled inferno.

Michelangelo! I'm addressing you,
you who remain in permanent strength;
No artist allows himself to be the victim
of any law, cool-blooded design,
to be the obeyer of traffic signs.
After the crucifixion, no trust in the world.
We glory in our own identity.

So, subversive painter of our condemnation,
painter of free souls to breathe and populate,
you knew the flesh that tore and shredded
through the nails was human;
we're cruelly trapped by faith.
Dormant seeds within the glorious ordinary.

A Calm Vacancy

No vacuous mindless mood, mind you.
This is deep business, a rise
from the almost-remembered smell of
a wet rugby ball on the Eden Park pitch,
the touch,
the feel of steel on the fighter cockpit's sides,
smell of oil, the height and symmetry
of the Norfolk Pines on Taupeka beach
in front of his grandmother's house.

Vague scrabble of emotions of
what's no longer carried on air
or felt with fingertips—the grab
and smash of thoughts.

A calm vacancy, an old man glimpsing absence
from across the room, limping into focus,
the oddly familiar figure growing closer
with a hardened mouth, offering something beyond,
something worth waiting for.

Michelangelo and the Pietà

> There can no more be a "Christian" art than there can be a Christian
> science . . . A painting of the Crucifixion is not necessarily more Christian
> in spirit than a still life, and may very well be less.
> —W.H. Auden, "Postscript: Christianity and Art"

I love this work more than the thump of
my own heartbeat. In the act, I dream deep
into a leaking heart, into profane stone
where, like buzzing flies, memory's mutterings come together.
The work is always confused, a confession of some kind
as the torso arises from flying chips, stone-dust.
It's a search for the destinations of a mother's love,
going beyond surface deception, trying to prevent this
being yet another of my lies.

No impulses arise, no fragile porcelain desires,
no muscles twisted as blue beech that could not
inform and crack the stone.
Only the straight grief-stare—the only distance,
the only direction a mother can find
as she holds a dead child born into death
between the breaths of the only love
that ever remains unchanged.

Stone is the place where one life ends, one begins.
The soul surfacing under my hands from within the stone.
I run fingers over her fingers, place the back of my hand
against her cheek. I chose to remain, to watch
her growing image burn hard onto the mind's plate
in this uncertain sift, this swither of inklings
becoming the work—my mother cradling me
at the beginning of my death, watching me
walk towards absence, singing.

It's Enough to Weather

Nature contains no negatives.
—Charles Wright, "China Traces"

I think life might be narrative.
We like to think that our stories
are our meaning. Memory is
a mixed cement of the important
with the unimportant,
engine of wear and tear.
Our job in this existence
is to recognize what matters.

But maybe we're just grain
groaning in chains of sea-fields,
breath exhaled into a breeze,
suddenly stiff, old,
disappearing by degrees
through the work of worms.
A line of time can't sum it up
or hold the juice of meaning.
I know I'll be another of the disappeared.
So, can you teach me how to love this?

Environmental Science

Night. Rain snitters on the half open window
of the Malmaison Hotel. According to the clock
it's not even five—too early to be awake.
I'm alone, straining to see out of the skylight,
feeling out of my depth, drowning,
unable to assume the world.

Against the lighted dock below trawlers
ride the pulse of the sea. The rustle of
drenched words, silver flash, spill
from baskets of tumbling tongues.
Leith men clatter, splash.
Clutter talk ricochets off hard stone
of wet cobbled courtyards between
the to and the fro of trade.
No consideration for the slow open space,
the necessary distance between rain drops,
the siren neon glistening.

In the dreich light, gulls and shore birds
whistle, scream songs and answers,
seeming somewhat misunderstood.
Tired to death, I stay put.

All day the living call till the ebb coal black,
the shrug-by-shrug of last light,
till the pub sign turns on night.
Then knitted songs of war from birds and men,
stories of dark atrocities descend again through
deep dark, the wild demonic space.
The moon has lost her mind.

In lonely hotel rooms, day or night,
sometimes we can just touch bottom
if we stand tiptoe.

Coleridge in Toronto

He's a heavy sleeper.
Behind his eyes he holds the stars
over Toronto, directionless webs
they seem to hang by nothing.
His world is a holograph,
carries the thing itself,
just as the spiral in a nautilus shell
carries the sea.
He is the windsweep off the lake,
marrying day with night, no gap between
Heaven and Hell, birth and death.
In his world it's no coincidence that
years are round, seasons come and go
and come again, everything spiralled
back through time.

Ahead, over the port lands, the sewage plant,
and beyond to Rochester, the universe collapses
by compass and square. Nothing apparent is
worth anything, the world an undiscovered metaphor.
Just the thing itself barrels on through the day.

In a hotel room on Queen's Quay, in a pants pocket,
"Kubla Khan" remains perfectly uncompleted.

Pangbourne Rain

For Alexander McCall Smith

The river is a slave girl
moving in sea-dreams,
who once danced wildly
for an ancient king.
She leaves something
of herself behind,
something of clouds
or other assignations.
Restrained, she is often
forgetful of her birth—
the pure freedom of rain.

A Painting of Angels

With acknowledgement to Charlie Maclean and Al Alvarez

> No one sings as purely as those who are in the deepest hell.
> Theirs is the song, which we confuse with that of the angels.
> —Franz Kafka

Melancholy shadows of Tuscan cedars
migrate across the lawn. Light touches.
Clouds alter. Heaven changes in the late sun.
Through incised windows the sudden chance
of shapes, the soft spread of mute wings—
the ghosts of holiness flying through the world.

The Lively Dead of Budle Hall

For Charlie MacLean

Jo tells her guests the garden is haunted.
This keeps the traffic down, gives her
a place of respite from visitors who take
over every corner of the house.
I'm out to grab a moment, a cigarette,
beyond the house-party crowd,
clear a space to work the way I have to.
I've turned out my pockets—left it all
to a coin toss in a moment of calm silence
in which poets live amongst sound.

Here my head is populated with traffic
of another kind, conversations, ghost voices:
children with ice cream; babbling, doting parents;
clinging lovers; menacing bastards stalking
the dark inner exchanges within earshot
of the sea's shout.
The night is stars as they never were before.
Out beyond the broken brick of the walled garden
wind-light streams from Holy Island, moans along
the curve of the surf line announcing some other
opening among worn, pockmarked gravestones.

This is rare society, figures made of memory.
I'm comforted by them. More than by those alive
whose shadowy crossings pass inside the windows
of the Hall where time calls and spirit is sometimes
rushed or ransacked by some ill-mannered misfit.

Leave me here to join the lively dead.

David Carradine Dead

Conversation between two women reading newspapers at Starbucks, June 5, 2009

"He hung himself in a Bangkok Hotel," she said.
The other, "Well, he was whacked out anyway."

No reasons—just "whacked out"
and gone—absence, news.

Somehow, I can tell neither of them can swim.

A Plea for the Ownership of Dogs

We're in it knee deep.
We forgot to make time go on forever . . .
left no one behind to wind the spring,
made nightmares out of faiths,
filled life with ripped rags captured
in minutes, diaries, letters, reports.
We so often miss the joke.

Crack your eggshell faith in all those permanent beliefs.
Think twice. Dig deep. Be strong. Courage! Try it!
Begin to love the deeper life of love in all its awkward,
frantic, ragged ways. I hope we all reach that point
of no return soon, that place that isn't safe.

Here's the measure of my vilification of you and me:
we can't shop our way out of this,
golf our way to a better score,
pull the power trip on our workmates for the boss's blessing,
beat the crap out of some stranger for the sheer hell of it.

The enemy is within.

How the World Completely Changes

This small truth an image expelled from your childhood.
—David Clink, "River of Words"

It became a winter when the past stayed,
when the young became old. Storm snow
dropped loosely from the meat of cold clouds.
The grip of stilled breath, the city silenced
under a cold-eyed sky. Hospital stacks
and factory roof vents poured buoyant steam.

It was one of those things, the type of change
that occurs everywhere. The Duncan McArthur
school bike stand stood tongue-frozen
in the teeth of half-light. The schoolyard white
linen-like, the snow packy enough for snowballs.
Snowball fights were against the rules, but we
asked the principal for an area to throw snow.
No girls allowed.

I caught one in the head.
The spit of melt trickled down my face.
Mr Hespeler called an end to it—
stood us in a row, a roaring red tongue,
a burning element in a black mouth.
But we're allowed to, we explained,
piling up snowballs during our detention.

In near-darkness, dimmed from the streetlights,
we lined up again. The stone-weight of his boot
crushing the pile—leaving us in shreds,
some kind of thinning, some change taking place.
I'm still sorry for the one thing I became sure of from
this dark age, though you might not want to hear it.
Growing up doesn't always slip in through the back door.

Windfall

> ... we glimpse the unity that we lost ...
> the forgotten astonishment of being alive.
> —Octavio Paz, "Sunstone"

I have this childhood windfall
stuffed in a drawer of my closet
in case something gives out—
I have a song, a beginning of a note,
just the very thing, the vital.
Picture a small kid, stubby fingers,
a handful of sand, the songs of
first birds of morning feeding the sea.

360 Degrees

For all our parents

> Earth, you darling . . .
> You were always right, and your holiest inspiration
> is Death, that friendly Death.
> Look, I am living . . .
> Supernumerous existence
> wells up in my heart.
> —Rilke, "The Ninth Elegy"

We saw your lives and paid for our own
in malevolence and lack of courage.
We invented, formed our worlds,
where most things don't matter.
Nursed our failure through meaningless faiths
in the struggle to be content.
Now we too grow slow into our faces,
fill out from outside in.
This end of our selves is our anthem.

We give up waiting.
No one has a clue about anything
though our fingerprints are all over everything.
A life of arrivals and departures, new love,
all these things of day-to-day
with which we filled in life.
Look, you don't need me to list them,
now so far away—though there's
reason for recollection that strikes
in sudden reflections of wrong judgments
in sullen store windows.

Forget hope.
It's time to negate time.
Gaze into space, look into the lens,
the beginning is the end.
Any physicist can tell you
God abolished himself.

Sometimes

I can't stand this grim compulsion.

Your victory howl drifts over long nights.

In spite of you, I live well.

I remember my breakdown in the south of France
and what those Mimosa blossoms did to your eyes.

Cider half-light is better than a muscular burning
so bright it brings the light of nothing to your retina.

Love must be found here, there'll be no comfort in the grave.

I know why trackmen swing their lamps.

As If

They left for work around 5:30 in the morning,
boots on Pine Street cobbles—the Irish from
the wrong side. We were Scots Prots on
Patrick Street, we lived surrounded.
Certain days, they paraded carrying swords.
Gran said it was to celebrate the killing of
Protestant boys. On those days, I wasn't
taking chances. I hid under the car with
Tommy and Francy Cosgrove. They figured
if I was under threat of death, they were too.
They were right. Their uncle Mike spanked them.
Many times I saw him carrying a sword in that parade.

The morning men repairing the brickwork
of the tannery stacks. Black stack-smoke
mixed with strains, grunt of trains at the station.
From my narrow attic window at number 142
I stepped into a world of senses.
It infected me in the way I would endure,
in trying to live at all with no screens on feeling.

This way of life still eats away at attempts
to re-tune the world. *You're a poet*, they say,
as if that excused enduring pain. As if
I could cure myself, fix it, didn't have to
bear the world's weight like everyone else,
or try to love its worth.

But God! If they're right,
I know whose side I'm on.

Whistling in the Dark

I

I'm aware of some who are writing
in the small hours of morning;
at a time of loss, the search for words,
their absence comes to me.
And the moon comes with secrets
jostled in the waves of window glass.
Silence between stars
threads the constellations.
The knife of this-and-that
has been discarded.

II

And when will the predicted snow
begin to fall, clothe the bones of maples,
be the only light in the unlight
where poems arise if it's not too late.

III

A stumble on the bed of night.
A sudden loss of cloaked hours.
The appearance of the scars of day-to-day.

IV

These sacred hours contain my hope
that this is how death will be—
the halt of the sun
allows us to alter the world.

BLOOD AND BONE

The Grammar of Distance

For my brother

We're making a trail in a silence of snow
that isn't ever going to heal. Our tracks
write a story in a language without words,
using a grammar of distance and blood.

Snowshoeing is difficult enough—breaking trail,
choosing a path through thick brush, over thin ice.
It's tough going. And all this exceeded by you,
following too closely, rabbiting on, talking
dropped threads—not waiting for replies.
Words as filler, words as distances, long years.

I've always done it, been the one
to break trail, carry the heaviest pack.
Always careful to have you follow me—
show you my back, make it easier.
Okay, more truthfully?
I can't handle what I find there.
There's weakness in this love.

Because I'm afraid to look you in the face;
I've tried to make you invisible.
Tried to cover you with a brave face
because you've never had the gift of a first kiss,
a boys' night out, a girl's desire you didn't
manufacture for yourself in that wounded mind.

In the end, it's been me unable to bear the unordinary.
No sunny corners in this that might make things easier.

Our trail is never going to heal over.
I apologize for my part in the world's cruelty.
To be honest brother, it dented me too.

Presqu'ile Beach in Winter

For my daughters

The sky is scraped steel wool.
Your mind raw, coming undone,
aware of the tension of the
small things that can't hide;
like you in this business of prophesy.
Everywhere you look you try to
calm the weather, move life's furnishings,
organize the world into that immaculate beginning—
but it's misbehaving in a spray of words.
You think, for a moment, all you have
is what you can nearly see.
Too strong to give up.
Too shattered to be mended.
That thought has you ashen-faced, sucking wind.

There is an edge where green jade waves
roar in, race out, uncover the beach, only to
cover it again . . . hesitation between each crest—
a glimpse of absence. In this no man's land of
continuous negotiation, a seagull floats
encased in ice, uninhabited cadaver,
a bitter death, a bird beached,
a bird off the hook.
You look for a stick to fish it out and
remember the kids in the sheen of summer.
Those days. Those times. The stoop
to scoop small waves with child fingers.

Amongst all the disturbing deaths of friends
that pile up these days, as though body after body
is being thrown into a pit for some mass burial,
the kids are necessary memories.

You know you can't stay with them, can't follow them,
but they're making the broken world as it once was.

The Slip Green of Remembering

For my mother

> This at least we should have
> the right to know before we leave,
> that dying we deprive the world of something whole.
> —Steven Heighton, "The Last Living Speaker"

Hush. We are in the centre of the world.
Hospital room, hourless time.
Emptied of words.
The inhalation of a last touch,
hand on hand before the melt of goodbye.

I watch her slip into a child face,
congealing into a death mask.
On the tip of her tongue her innocence,
a ribbon in her child hair,
playing "Club" in the shed.
The slip green of remembering.
Her father's telling eyes as when
he died and she was fourteen.
Hard stones of time and place—
a last wearing of her face again
weathered to paper-thin skin.

We don't mourn the dead. There is
a ceaseless mill of anyone's dying.
I see her in Summerhill Park, stooped
over a drift of Norwegian poppies,
under complaints of street lamps and
shitting dogs, advice over coffee stains
on my coat. In my green stem of stories

she will continue to slip, until by my death
of memory the tragedy will begin,
the world will be deprived.

A Confession of Birds

Inside, we feel the terror of dusk begin.
Outside we watch the evening, failing again,
and we let it happen. We can say nothing.
—Simon Armitage, "November"

Becoming aware of how much longer life
had been for my father made me watch him
scan the evening sky. A confession of birds
flew overhead as death-high two hawks climbed
on wires of spirals. One relaxed, paused,
folded its wings, plummeted into the ground,
lay stone dead.

Did a heart give out, give up, tire?
My speculations didn't interest my old man.
He was thin, skin-weathered, leaning against his
bent back, putting a last mile on the clock, waiting.
It was as if his smile was imagined.
In other days he wouldn't have been willing
to take it lying down. Now he was willing
to be someone else. I didn't like it one bit.
Any of it.

I never did get any reasons why.
And my father died without ever
referring to one thing or the other.
But since the fatal fall, I've been
longing for some explanation—
other than a giving out, an inheritance
other than final failure.

Elegy for My Father

> Nothing rose to the occasion after that.
> —Seamus Heaney, "Wheels Within Wheels"

Nothing came close to lifting the weight
of life like that; nothing rose to its height—
the sly smile, the tight fist of hot youth,
a prince in skies, senses tuned by fear,
moving on wings of wind.

Fly it by feel, by the seat of your pants,
a 350-mile-per-hour fighter,
1,350-horsepower Merlin engine.
A human frame strapped to thin steel.
The judder of cannon-cracks, smacks of shells,
tracer lights of Christmas,
another smack on the heavy glass above his head.
The smoke, roll, sudden flash fireball.
A tiny body falls from Angels 3 into
the heavens of the sea.

All these years a stiffening life surfaced from DNA
only a heavy stare away from cold dead friends
in rolling black foam, sea-wreath waves,
dark sea-wreath shadows around his eyes.

Tonight some guy has closed the coffin lid.
I'm left with you, leaning into those
endless days of family. Up a steep flight
of another kind, the staircase of you—
wearing your old coat for a little too long
because a son needed new skates, a guitar.
As if my lost causes ever really mattered.

Star-thrower

For O

Demanding to be born, she was born
with excessive force, a caul intact, a cry.
The midwife fussed, *She's inconsolable.*
She's a seer.
She knows something the rest of us don't.
On the islands there are perfect loves
born like this that can't be lived on earth.
Something will keep her as far as the moon.

And she was always leaving, absenting herself,
stretching her branches up from the top of
Dundreich Hill behind Earlyvale House
to be inducted into the sky again.
Not seeming a child.
Always doing hard labour.
She could predict the weather.
Speak the language of roe deer.
Find fish swimming through rain.
She knew about lifetimes.

The child knew her physics—about our
relationship to the birth and death of stars,
how we are made and of what,
knew sorrow's weight from birth,
that anvil thrown into her lap.
She knew what Scots have always known:
All your life you'll dance when you
lay grief down—but you'll pick it up again
when the music ends.

Concerning grief, she once told me,
Though it's unsafe, poetry will always be written
because of what it is. And once she counselled me
on finding a new career.
Only to make a living, of course, I said,
thinking of my work. She didn't respond,
being suddenly far away as the moon.

Michiko and the POW

For Aunt Michiko, who survived Hiroshima

Bare feet on the searing heat of the oven,
forced to stand, weighted down forced to
hold buckets of bricks. Then, knees to his chin, folded,
imprisoned within a fish trap and speared with bamboo sticks.
After the war, after a time, he forgave a brother
for marrying "that Jap" whose own wounds
his brother lay beside every night,
holding her so as not to lift burned flesh
off cancerous, smoking bones,
kissing lips tasting of brackish water,
crushed coal, her mouth an entry
to some deep, exhausted mine.

After she'd inhaled the bomb, her skin
healed into leather and lava. There she
mapped the mysterious territory of the heart,
a military campaign, a guide
for the crew of the *Enola Gay*.

For my father, she drew another map—
contour lines, historical sites clearly marked,
boundary lines revised.
Showed him how to love.

Best Friends

In memory of D.S.

Your silence is a sudden heat loss without explanation.
We have to resolve this leaving.
I can't believe our argument was that serious.
I'm not taking all the blame.
But this puts me up against it.
I've given you everything I have.
Or, at least, everything I could have.

Hazardous to take our usual walk past the treeline—
hang aloft on the tight ledge above the glen as we used to.
But I'm not giving up the habit of almost twenty years
because I might run into you.

I'm still waiting. Still shocked.
Spilled like wreckage across the shoulder of the hill
from what was left unsaid.
You've left me with a dead weight.
Why should I have to contend with that?
Hey! Listen to me. Hear me out.
I'm talking to you!
Whatever you're saying, I can't hear.
I can't read between the lines.

At this point, I didn't care if I was
making a scene, banging, shouting
through the coffin lid, closed
because he had put a gun to his ear
and blown his bloody brains out.

The Battle of a Cold Night

I know my location. I'm at the farm.
But tonight on dark edges of remote cosmic things,
in this frame of mind, this general panic,
I have to ask where I am—try to resist
the urge to make a break for it.
This sudden stranding is a real handful.
The familiar fence lines,
the thick edge of the trees,
even the pole star,
none of these provide answer or direction.

A lot of men would just live through it,
but rumours continue to grow
while a slow gloom of dark indigo
rolls over the ribs of snow fields
and the night becomes a sea-surge of stars.
My heart is pounding and will explode
in a ball of flesh, blood, and bone
if I don't find a way out of this.
Something has to give.

Then a deep cadence places a finger on
my heartbeat, soft as caution, saying:
Spirit, this is your compass point,
your wind-rose, your direction—
you are leaving this life.
Now live with that.

Evidence at Pompeii

In the back alleys behind the shops
asses sat and bowels strained.
A loom weight is found,
a leather shoe, a smoking pipe,
the bones of a baby—dark secret
wrapped in parchment—
the drawing of his neighbour's wife
to which he masturbated
for a whole month
fuelled by memory's flesh.

We uncover black pits
of self-consuming fires.
Leave evidence of our lives
in spite of worms—evidence
of the now becoming then,
a past that shells and grows around us
as we sit with our backs to history.
Of love itself, we leave no clues.

The Language of the Dead

Atoms of history . . . vaporize into the lungs.
Hold it there. You are keeping
yourself in breath . . . You are breathing the past.
Make it real again, because
this is the cycle to which we are all born.
—Simon Armitage, "Killing Time"

Words can be lost, but these ruins carry murmurs
that grow to show the range of the human voice.
We're knee-deep in the dead.
Here we look for new perspectives—
bits and bobs of the forgotten day-to-day
found and forgotten again.
The archeologists recover memories in places
where tourists don't go: dumps, middens,
the mounds of wise garbage,
the buried evidence of unchanging symptoms.
Even the dust is flesh from death.
Sloughed skin coats the walls in a black scale of human cells
like the tunnels of London's Underground.
We breathe it.

Everything flows from the same source, the same
day after day, some of it spoken, thought, unthinkable—
babies dying of crib death; men and women arguing,
gesturing, waving from the miscommunications of kitchens,
dinners made by a maid taking up the rope of the unspoken
household strain, bathrooms full of primping girls; mirrors
speaking to some woman who looks great in red,
makeup sold in shops (she's applying the truth about mascara
and charcoal for a night's seduction); bowls broken
by the anger of a frustrated wife, tossing

the timeless graffiti when she comes unstuck.
In the profound absence you can hear that shout
from the terrible weight of living,
though no mouths move.
Fill your lungs.
We are as tragic as our history.
Nothing's changed.
Our lives burned before.

The Fight in My Fist

> . . . and there fires begin . . .
> —George MacKay Brown

Strathnaver's scenery isn't improving my mood,
it's entering me. Inheritance.
A recognition of infected past.
My family of MacKay was murdered here.
I'm thinking about those I know, the way
everything can be justified; it's for the best,
God's will, when I know we are measured by loss;
that's the promise of age.
And I'm sick of being piled high from debts to all of you.
There's a collision in this citizenship.

We drive through Langall, Syre, Kidsary.
I chant the villages like Hail Marys—
the names a rosary of grief.
Hills rise higher with sacrifice.
I hear my voice utter stones of words.
I think how the deep weight of the present
is ours to decipher in the bone's marrow.

We stop for tea and a break. Eagles spiral above
as we lean against the wall of the graveyard
balancing mugs on the thin stone top.
Against the surge of hills, ghost figures
trudge before the hiss of a burning sky,
stumble towards us, children—thin-boned,
bent heads and shawls, low sobs, too tired to cry.
And men, fire-branded, black ash tears,
walk towards absence, leaving old women
pain-clenched in beds, women who taste

the wild honey of past kisses in cindered mouths,
women who sit all day in nests of flame—
widow wicks, melted candles,
the hiss of human fat and flesh
until they simply smoke like peat.

Something beats in the very bone of the heart.
But I have no understanding of this.
All I have is a fight in my fist.

Uneven

We are as uneven as Foucault's pendulum is true,
hanging in imbalance. Each hesitant wave forms
and breaks on the beach. Each arrhythmic pulse
a private wound for our eyes only. So, at any moment,
we move one way or another in transitional space
where feelings swing.
At one end, we're pushed together in xanthic light
in skin-tight knowledge of each other. At the other,
we try desperately to do the impossible—
keep to ourselves.

Timeless

The country of self is abandoned.
A friend has died; another gone whereabouts
to look with the exile's privilege
(from the outside in)
through watchful silence.

Left behind, I stare eye to eye,
hear behind a heartsick voice
inklings and oddments of feeling
(words no longer the scaffold of meaning).
A heart now understands in all patterns of loss
love is the flesh of life.

In the intimacy of dreams
the still sad music of humanity sings.
Amongst murmurs of a supreme theme
a candle fights to stay alive—
triumphs over wreckage by its gleam.

In absence, they become pure conscience,
the voices of feelings I summon far inland.
They don't need to clear a calendar.
They simply arrive without a knock
and enter through the unlocked door.

The Island of Iona

For Sir Max MacLeod in honour of his father, Lord MacLeod, the preserver of a holy place

All islands are holy places;
You cannot be surrounded by sea
And not pray.
—Roland Leach, "Islands"

Under these skies, standing stones
call lightning onto the head
of a holy man in the flames of exile,
set fire to the world.

Pilgrims who arrive by bus and ferry
from Craignure journey ashore
leaving personal effects behind.
They carry no name, no history,
no longer citizens, having lost nothing.
They're alone on their own terms,
free from departing.
Here they live among Macbeth,
other dead kings, and the Word engraved on rocks
by the sea's skin—ocean out, ocean in.

In a language that calls out the unexamined,
MacLeod prays for the dead as nails.
The living screams naked;
a terrible mouth in the fist of his face,
electrified by the burning cold of morning sea.
This beast reveals solace and anger
in the bitter deep of days.

All the Poets in the Bar

For Ned Hagerman

> Under the surface of flux and of fear there is an underground movement
> . . . the Kingdom of individuals . . . loyal by intuition, born to attack, and
> innocent.
> —Louis MacNeice, "The Kingdom"

At our age we don't take comfort in past steps.
We don't matter anymore.
We almost stood the test of time;
but then, life was never up to us.
Yet look at the company we keep on Harbord Street.
The music still sweeps us off our feet.
It's steps that exist in the mind
as words which dance and rhyme
that matter most.

Listen to the silence, stillness.
How innocent it seems at 2 a.m.
The birds in the park have bent their heads.
They don't call anymore. They're busy being;
the rest they can do without.

My friend, your god has already saved us—
keeps us stocked with the surprises that keep us living.
He's the words beyond any cords that tie your hands,
rags that staunch bleeding, the solar wind's whisper-hiss
in broad spaces between stars. He's the time that remains
timeless when spring is still easy as snowballs and boys.

Where are you going? Home?
What are you going to think after this conversation?
Is there anything to do? No?
Home sounds like a good place,
not far from our kingdom of individuals.
And sleep, like death, sounds close to truth.

Return

It's become more and more difficult to be lost,
to be as I have always been, unclaimed
and unclaiming any origin.
Beneath the scrape of luggage and ownership of things,
a self in the country of self.
A new place pretends to bring a new self,
but it's only the old set free.
I have chosen to be a foreigner.
I have chosen separation.

Why is it the landmarks I recognize only in memory,
imbued with that past mood or the weather that I felt
on my skin, the details of a café I was in, church,
house, the streets, are lost to me?
The mood is the meaning; the memory of place
lies in the senses—visions of liberty.

When I return, any sadness I feel
is from what has died of the place I knew
when everything that was, was there.
Though the place is in some ways the same,
breathing a tangle of strange and familiar,
it has floated away in my absence.

Exodus and Exile

> All our efforts must tend toward the light.
> —Antonio Machado

Couples have drifted home to beds.
On the walls opposite the café, cats make
large shadows with their lives. The ending
of night tastes like something lost. A slow music
in the clink of stays as boats float on the pulse
of the sea. Pearl lights thread through olive trees
along the quays to fight the dark. Silence is
wrapped in almonds, olives, mimosa-scented shades.
No comings and goings in Collioure.
The lid of night nailed down.

The café owner knows I'm on his watch tonight,
and this one will end with the dark.
He's been serving solitude by the glass,
starts to count his cash,
accuses me of having lost love, of being alone.
Tells me to finish, go home.
But you know it's options you've lost.
It's over. She's gone. You're alone.

Birds are beginning to sing connection in the graphite
light, asking who made it to this murmur of morning.
The call's a harsh reminder—it's an even tougher question.

NOTES

Music of a Walk Through Leaves
The title refers to Vita Sackville-West's description of the perfect sound of happiness, the sound made while walking through fallen leaves, which became a family term for anything wonderful—it was said to be "through leaves."

The Snow Garden at Massey College
Massey College is a private independent college located on the campus of the University of Toronto. Thanks to the generosity of the current Master, Dr John Fraser, it has been a refuge for me. Many of these poems have been written within its walls.

This May Not Be Love
This poem was inspired by the lines, "But said some things and never meant them / sweet nothings anybody could have mentioned," by Simon Armitage in "To His Lost Lover." The phrase "traffic of her stare" comes from someone else, but I can't attribute it.

Shoot the Moon
The katydid is a large iridescent green insect that is attracted to light at night. It is found in Canada and rasps to proclaim territory and to search for a mate.

The Falcon
The images and vocabulary come from the ancient sport of falconry:

To *mantle*—to stand over a kill with wings lowered and spread to hide the food
To *tower*—to soar up and hover looking for prey

To man—to tame a falcon by accustoming it to a human
  presence
Unmanned—free and wild

The Mill at Eyrland
The title refers to the ancient mill located in the Orkney Islands near Stromness. A mill has likely stood in that location for thousands of years. "The buttered moon," or words similar to that, is an image of Orkney poet, George MacKay Brown.

The Walk to Plockton Cemetery
Sorley MacLean, the Gaelic poet and makar of the Clan MacLean, died and was buried in 1996 on the Isle of Skye near where he lived. Although he was eighty-five when he died, his death came as a shock to his friends. When I knew him, he was serving as Headmaster of a school in Plockton, a small village on the west coast of Scotland. He won many awards for his poetry, including the Queen's Medal for Poetry, and was nominated for a Nobel Prize for Literature. Curiously, and by accident, some forty years later my daughter became a roommate of Sorley's granddaughter in Edinburgh.

The Michelangelo Code
The line, "that baffling space" comes from Barry Dempster. The line, "that gap between the flesh and the turtle's shell" is an unknown borrowed description. The line, "the infection of Sin and Stern Repentance" comes from William Blake, "The Marriage of Heaven and Hell."

A Calm Vacancy
Eden Park and Taupeka are places of my father's childhood in New Zealand.

Michelangelo and the Pietà
This poem is written for my mother. And it was inspired by these words by W.H. Auden:

So long as an activity is regarded as being of sacred importance, it is controlled by notions of orthodoxy . . . But once art becomes a secular activity, every artist is free to treat whatever subject excites his imagination, and in a stylistic manner which he feels appropriate.
—"Postscript: Christianity and Art"

All fabrication (making) is an imitation of motherhood.
—"Genius and Apostle"

Environmental Science
The line "unable to assume the world" is a direct reference to T.S. Eliot's line in the poem "Preludes": "impatient to assume the world."

Coleridge in Toronto
It is known that Coleridge always carried a copy of "Kubla Khan" in his pocket. He claimed the writing of the poem, remembered upon awakening from a dream, was interrupted by a visit from "the man from Porlock" and never completed. It is likely that the "visitor" never existed. In my view, and in the view of many Coleridge scholars, the poem is complete.

The Lively Dead of Budle Hall
Budle Hall is a country house on the shores of Budle Bay across the water from Holy Island and Lindisfarne. It is the home of my friends Jo and David Coates, to whom I was introduced by Charles MacLean. This poem is a new version of an earlier one published in *The Stone Skippers*. Holy Island is the site of the ancient monastery of

Lindisfarne. It is populated by the mounds of the dead—monks slain by Viking raiders in the ninth century CE.

The Grammar of Distance

This poem was written for my brother, Ron. The title of this poem, and of the book itself, is taken from a poem by Scots poet, John Burnside, published in the *Times Literary Supplement* in 2008, ". . . that grammar of distance and blood" (John Burnside, "Alcools"). The lines "Our tracks / write a story in a language without words" come from Tomas Transtromer's "March 1979": ". . . deer-slots in the snow: a language, / language without words."

Elegy for My Father

My father, a Royal Navy, Fleet Air Arm, Senior Pilot, and carrier fighter squadron commander during the Second World War, was decorated twice "for conspicuous bravery and gallantry in the face of the enemy" in 1944. He was nominated a third time for a bar to his Distinguished Service Cross by his CO in February 1945 for his Arctic service on the Murmansk convoys. His death, suggested by this poem, is exaggerated.

Michiko and the POW

Forgive the storyteller for trying and lying to try to explain the truth about the horrible complexities of war and peace. While my father did lose friends to the cruelty of the Japanese guards in POW camps, some by beheading, he did not feel anything but love for his sister-in-law. But after the war, in New Zealand, for reasons she understood and accepted and forgave, she was often badly treated by the population. She was indeed a Hiroshima survivor.

The Language of the Dead

The line, "the truth about mascara" comes from Simon Armitage's poem "At Sea." The black scale on the walls of the London Underground comprises dead skin cells (dust) sloughed off in the natural way of things by passengers. "Our lives have burned before" is a line from a poem by Molly Peacock.

The Fight in My Fist
My great-great-great-grandparents and our extended family of MacKay were driven out of Strathnaver in what was one of the most vicious chapters in the history of the Highland Clearances. Some in my family were killed by Sellars and his men, agents of the Duke of Sutherland, who torched their homes and villages. Many of my family who survived made their way to Orkney. I acknowledge the source of images that arose from my reading of the works of George MacKay Brown

Timeless
This poem is for Michael Roberts and Alexander McCall Smith.

The Island of Iona
This poem is written for Sir Maxwell McLeod, whose father, Lord MacLeod, rebuilt the monastery on the ancient site of the island of Iona and made it once again into a place of pilgrimage and prayer. He was well known throughout the world as a remarkable preacher and learned scholar.

All the Poets in the Bar
This poem is written for the poet Ned Hagerman. Harbord Street is the location of Harbord House Pub where landlord John Oakes welcomes poets and writers who participate in a reading series held there each month.

Return
This poem is based on Alistair Reid's *Notes on Being a Foreigner*.

Exodus and Exile

This poem was written in Collioure, France, where the great Spanish poet, Antonio Machado, died shortly after the long march out of Barcelona to escape Franco and the fascists. This poem is modelled on his translated poetry.

ACKNOWLEDGEMENTS

A number of the poems included in *The Grammar of Distance* have appeared in such publications as *The New Quarterly*, *Contemporary Verse 2*, *Prairie Fire*, *Jones Avenue*, and *poetry'zown*.

The Grammar of Distance was edited by Catherine Graham. I thank her for her patience, advice, support, and honesty.

For their help, advice, and support, I thank Alexander McCall Smith, Charles MacLean, Lois Lorimer, Ned Hagerman, Mel Wiebe, Shirarose Wilensky, Jack MacLeod, Kildare and Linda Dobbs, Scott Griffin, Master John Fraser (Massey College), A.F. Moritz, always Halli Villegas, and my wife, Catherine West.

The cover art is *Shipboard Morning* by Linda Kooluris Dobbs. I thank Linda for her generosity and support.

ABOUT THE AUTHOR

Ian Burgham is an associate of the League of Canadian Poets. Born in New Zealand and raised in Canada, he has lived and worked in New Zealand and Scotland. He studied literature at Queen's University and at the University of Edinburgh. He worked as an editor for Canongate Publishing and later became publisher of Macdonald Publishing in Edinburgh. He has previously published two collections of poetry, *A Confession of Birds*, a chapbook published in the UK in 2004, and *The Stone Skippers*, published in 2007 by Tightrope Books and nominated for the Relit Award in 2008. He currently divides his time between Toronto and Kingston. In 2004–5 Burgham won the Queen's University "Well-Versed" Poetry Award. Since then, his work has been published in many Canadian literary journals including *Prairie Fire, Contemporary Verse 2, The New Quarterly, Literary Review of Canada, Queen's Quarterly, dANDelion, Harpweaver, PRECIPICe, Jones Avenue, poetry'zown*, and *Ascent Aspirations*.